Guido Ludes · Venedig Venezia Venice

Venedig Guido Ludes
Venezia
Venice

Mit einem Vorwort von Nevia Pizzul Capello

Textauswahl von Hermann Kurzke

Herausgegeben von Michael Reitzel

Verlag Hermann Schmidt Mainz 1996

Vorwort

Ein „Venedig als Geisteszustand" legt uns Guido Ludes vor, der dem glänzenden Blau eines triumphierenden Sommers die graue Unterbrechung der winterlichen Nebel gegenüberstellt, die Eintönigkeit des Regens, die im Dunst verstärkten Laute, das regelmäßige Widerhallen auf dem feuchten Pflaster.

Einer einfühlsamen Auswahl von Autoren, die den Winter in Venedig geatmet haben und dieser Stadt in einer düsteren Zeit schöne Seiten gewidmet haben, entnimmt er Verse, die wie ein Blitzlicht aufflammen und kommentargleich die Bilder erhellen. Und in ihrem Gefolge wird Ludes zum Poeten, er begleitet uns die Fondamenta entlang, an denen die Gondeln vor sich hin dämmern; er führt uns durch Fluchten von Gassen, die sich im Unendlichen verlaufen; hinauf auf die Altane des Ghettos, wie ein neuer Melchisedek Rilkes. Von oben scheint alles rings umher dunkel, gedämpft, strichweise von einem flüchtigen Schimmer umschmeichelt, der unbeweglich einen Augenblick lang innehält und dann weiterfliegt, weit weg, über die steinerne Stadt hinaus, einem friedlichen silbernen Licht entgegen: dem Meer, dem von einer beherrschenden Stadt verführten Verführer, von einer Stadt, die seit einem Jahrtausend ihr Leben mit ihm verbindet.

Zum Meer hin erstreckt sich der Canal Grande mit seinem undurchdringlichen Wasser. Die Palette der Vedutenmaler ist mit Schlamm verschmiert, mit braunen schleimigen Algen, mit Teerflecken, die die Boote hinterlassen: das Hellblau, das Grün, das Kobaltblau sind eins mit dem dunklen Grau, das in den „Notturni" ins tiefste Schwarz übergeht, wo die Stadt aus dem Wasser entsteht, vom Widerschein erleuchtet, sich düster aufrichtet, wie auf der Hut, ein Bollwerk gegen das drohende Meer. An der weiten Biegung des Kanals treffen wir das „letzte Linienboot", ebenfalls mit ausgeschalteten Lichtern, geräuschlos, bateau fantôme des dritten Jahrtausends, und seine langsame Fortbewegung sagt uns, daß zumindest jemand am Steuer stehen muß, ein Lebenszeichen, das sich abhebt von der dunklen Unbeweglichkeit der Paläste, deren Fenster wie leere Augenhöhlen offenstehen.

Und der feuchte, hauchdünne Nebel, die eisige Feuchtigkeit dringt uns in die Knochen. Das ist Venedig im Winter, von November bis Januar, mit seinem Nebel, seinem Hochwasser: eine Stadt, die Sehnsucht hervorruft, die ihre Träume in die Garnwinde des Gedächtnisses einflicht.

Und die Zeichnungen von Guido Ludes? Durchgehende Striche, die nach unten stürzen, in einem grandiosen Fall, die den nächtlichen Himmel erleuchten, oder die, der Schwerkraft folgend, fallen und die Seele in freudigem und mystischem Schwung nach oben freilassen. Das Bild scheint die verborgenen

Kräfte, die im Kosmos schlummern und vor der Zeit aus dem Leben in den Schoß der Ewigkeit zurückkehrten, ausbrechen zu lassen. Diese Arbeiten von Ludes werden zu einem kleinen architektonischen Meisterwerk, wenn zu dem zögernden und verträumten Ton die bewußte Kunst des klaren Schnitts, der sicheren Unterbrechung, der kunstvollen Wiederaufnahme kommt. Dieses architektonische Verfahren, das durchaus berechnend scheinen mag, ist in Wirklichkeit schwerelos, von einer Melodie durchzogen, die im Bild verweilt wie eine verhallende Note, offen ins Unbegrenzte.

Bei Ludes scheint die romantische Sehnsucht aus der Betrachtung der Stadt zu entstehen, aus der Überraschung der ersten Begegnung, der Entdeckung, die als innere und sentimentale Subjektivität vorherrscht, überwältigt von der umgebenden Natur: Wasser, Licht, Widerschein, Lagune, Verherrlichung des Lebens und seines Gegenteils, einer Sache, die stirbt, um wieder aufzustehen: das Sein als Läuterung. Und dieses Venedig wird in der Umklammerung des Winters zum Symbol dafür, indem es - als erneuerter Ceresmythos - im Dualismus Licht-Schatten den Dualismus Leben-Tod darstellt. Der Tod ist das andere. Wie in keiner anderen Stadt ist der Tod hier an das Leben gebunden: durch das Zusammenspiel und die ständige Änderung der Stile und der unterschiedlichen künstlerischen Ausdrucksformen, Darstellung einer aristokratischen Üppigkeit und einer würdevollen Armut, die sich ohne Unterbrechung in den Fassaden der auf engem Raum aneinandergeschmiegten Paläste, Läden, Häuser abwechselt.

Bei Ludes verbindet der starke durchgehende Strich Paläste und Kirchen, als symbolischer Topos für Übergang und Rückkehr, als Verbindung zwischen dem Diesseits und dem Jenseits. Das grafische Zeichen stellt eine Beziehung her, ein Netz mit materiellen und immateriellen Berührungspunkten zwischen der Energie des Künstlers und anderen im Raum schwebenden Energien.

Für dieses „cimmerio" ist Venedig der Ort der mystischen und künstlerischen Betrachtung, ist es der Beginn der ständigen Metamorphose, die Leben bedeutet. Das Venedig in Schwarzweiß von Guido Ludes wird lebendig in der bebenden Zuneigung des Autors und empfängt materielle Wärme durch seine Hand. Es wird das Charakteristikum eines Künstlers auf der Suche nach ewigen lyrischen Werten, das von der geheimnisvollen Beziehung zwischen dem Menschen und den Dingen erzählt, die er vergeistigt und der er, indem er sie benennt, eine ontologische Wirklichkeit verleiht.

„Mein Venedig geht nicht unter", betitelt Guido Ludes eine Zeichnung, eine beschwörende Aussage, die wie eine Verheißung wirkt.

NEVIA PIZZUL CAPELLO, VENEDIG

Introduzione

Una „Venezia-stato d'animo" ci propone Guido Ludes, che alle giornate smaltate d'azzurro del trionfo estivo antepone la grigia pausa delle nebbie invernali, la monotonia della pioggia, suoni amplificati nella caligine, cadenze ritmate sul selciato umido.

Da una sensibile scelta letteraria di autori che hanno respirato l'inverno a Venezia, dedicando a questa città, in una fase opaca, belle pagine, egli trae i versi che come flash si accendono ad illuminare le sue immagini, quasi un commento. E Ludes, sulla loro scorta, si fa poeta e ci accompagna lungo fondamenta alle quali s'intravedono attraccate gondole sonnacchiose; ci guida in una fuga di calli che si perdono all'infinito ci solleva sulle altane del Ghetto, nuovi Melchisedec di Rilkiana memoria. Dall'alto le cose intorno sembrano oscure, smorzate, lambite a tratti da fugaci bagliori che le accarezzano, sostando immobili sopra di esse, ma per un attimo, per poi riprendere il volo che li porterà lontano, oltre la città di pietra, verso una luce pacata ed argentea: il mare, seduttore sedotto da una città domina-captiva, che lega ad esso, da un millennio, la sua esistenza.

Al mare tende il Canal Grande con le sue acque cupe. La tavolozza dei Vedutisti si è inzuppata di fango, di brune alghe limacciose, di chiazze bitumose per lo scarico delle imbarcazioni: l'azzurro, il verde, il cobalto si sono miscelati ad un opaco grigiore che trapassa nel nero più profondo nei „notturni", dove la città nasce dall'acqua, illuminandosi di riflessi o ergendosi tetra, quasi all'erta, baluardo contro l'impendente minaccia del mare. All'ampia curva del Canale ci si imbatte nel „ultimo vaporetto" di linea, anch'esso spento, anch'esso silenzioso, bateau fantôme del Terzo millennio che ci fa intuire, dal lento avanzare almeno qualcuno al suo timone, un segno di vita che contrasta l'oscura immobilità dei palazzi dalle finestre spalancate come orbite vuote.

E questa nebbia sottile, impalpabile, questo gelido umidore ci penetra nelle ossa. Questa è la Venezia invernale, che ritroviamo da novembre a gennaio, con le sue brume, con le sue acque alte: una città evocatrice di nostalgia, che intesse i suoi sogni all'arcolaio della memoria.

E i designi di Guido Ludes?: incessanti tratti di matita che precipitano verso il basso, in una caduta gloriosa, illuminando il cielo notturno, o cadono, per peso d'inerzia, liberando in un gioioso e mistico slancio l'anima verso l'alto. L'immagine sembra voler far erompere le forze inesplicate che dormono nel cosmo, rientrate anzitempo dalla vita nel grembo dell'eternità. Questi lavori di Ludes diventano un piccolo capolavoro architettonico allorchè al tono esitante e trasognato si sovrappone una consapevole arte dei tagli netti, delle ferme pause, delle sapienti riprese. Tale

procedimento architettonico, che può sembrare anche troppo calcolato, è in realtà scevro di pesantezza, percorso anzi da una linea melodica che resta nell'immagine come una nota musicale sospesa, aperta verso l'illimitato.

In Ludes, il sentimento romantico della Sehnsucht sembra nascere nella contemplazione della città, nella sorpresa del primo incontro, nella scoperta che s'impone quale soggettività intima e sentimentale, commossa dalla natura dell'ambiente: acqua, luce, riflessi, la laguna, l'esaltazione della vita e del suo contrapposto, di qualcosa che muore in attesa di rinnovarsi: un senso catartico dell'esistenza, di cui questa Venezia, cinta dall'abbraccio dell'inverno, diventa simbolo, riproponendo - novello mito di Cerere - nella dualità luce-tenebre, la dualità vita - morte. La morte è differenza. Come in nessun'altra città, la morte è qui legata alla vita per quel coesistere e continuo mutare di stili, di espressioni artistiche diverse, manifestazioni di aristocratica opulenza e di dignitosa povertà, che si alternano senza soluzione di continuità nelle facciate dei palazzi, delle botteghe, delle case, addossantesi le une agli altri, quasi incalzati dallo spazio esiguo.

In Ludes la traccia rafforzata e continua del suo segno congiunge palazzi e chiese, come topos simbolico del passaggio e del ritorno, come legame tra l'al-di-qua e l'al-di-là. Il suo gesto grafico diventa pertanto relazione, rete di contatti materiali ed immateriali fra l'energia dell'artista ed ogni altra energia fluttuante nello spazio. Per questo „Cimmerio" Venezia è luogo di contemplazione mistica ed artistica, è principio della metamorfosi perenne, che è vita. La Venezia in bianco-nero di Guido Ludes è vivificata dal trepido affetto del suo autore, riscaldata dal calore materiale della sua mano. Essa diventa la cifra di un artista alla ricerca di valori lirici eterni, che parla dei rapporti misteriosi tra l'uomo e le cose, che egli spiritualizza e, nominandole, conferisce loro una realtà ontologica.

„La mia Venezia non sprofonda", intitola Guido Ludes un suo disegno: un'affermazione scaramantica che ha il valore di una promessa.

NEVIA PIZZUL CAPELLO, VENEZIA

Preface

What Guido Ludes here presents to us is a "Venice as a spiritual mood", confronting the shining blue of a triumphant summer with the grey interval of winterly fogs, the monotony of the rain, the sounds intensified by the mist, and the rhythmic cadences on the moist pavement. From a strikingly sensitive selection of authors, who breathed the Venetian winter and who dedicated beautiful pages to this city in a gloomy time, Ludes takes verses which light up and illuminate his pictures with a flash, just like a comment. And in the wake of those lines, Ludes becomes a poet; he accompanies us along the "fondamenta" where gondolas doze; he leads us through rows of lanes vanishing into infinity, up to the balconies of the ghetto – just like a new Melchisedech by Rilke. From above, all the things around look dark, subdued, touched here and there by a soft, gleaming shimmer that seems to caress them, then, without moving, pauses for a moment and finally flies away, far away beyond the stones of Venice, towards a peaceful, silvery light: to the sea, the temptress tempted by a dominating city, a city whose life has been linked to the sea for a thousand years.

With its opaque waters, the Grand Canal reaches out to the sea. The palettes of the Vedute painters get smeared with mud, with brown, slimy alga, with tar spots left by the passing boats: the light blue, the green, the cobalt blue blend together with the darkish grey which turns into the deepest black in the "notturni" where the city emerges from the water, illuminated by reflection, and rises sombrely – as if she were on her guard, a bastion against the threatening sea. At the wide curve of the canal we meet "the last regular boat" with its lights turned off too, without a sound, a bateau fantôme of the third millennium; and its slow locomotion suggests that there must be somebody at the helm, a sign of life which contrasts with the obscure motionlessness of the palaces whose windows gape open like empty eye sockets.

And the damp, extremely thin fog, this icy humidity penetrates our bones. This is Venice in winter, from November till January, with her fog, her flooding; a city which evokes nostalgia, twining her dreams into a web of memories.

And the drawings of Guido Ludes? Straight strokes, precipitating downwards in a brilliant fall; strokes, which illuminate the sky at night or, following gravity, fall right down and release the soul in a joyful and mystic leap upwards. The pictures seem to let hidden powers free, which, having returned from life into the lap of eternity long ago, are now asleep in the cosmos. These works by Ludes become little architectonic masterpieces, whenever his reticent, dreamy tone is joined by the deliberate art of clear cuts, confident breaks, and artful reversions. This architectonic

procedure – which appears to be positively calculating – is actually weightless, pervaded by a melodious line which lingers with the picture like a note dying away into boundlessness.

In Ludes, romantic feelings of yearing seem to arise from the contemplation of the city, the surprise felt at the first encounter, the discovery which distinguishes itself by precisely this intimate and sentimental subjectivity, overwhelmed by the nature of the surrounding ambience: water, light, reflections, the lagoon, the glorification of life and its counterpart, something which dies in order to rise again – a purifying sense of existence. All this is epitomised by the city of Venice which, enfolded in a winterly embrace, unfolds into the symbol of a new Ceres myth, picturing the dualism of life and death within the dualism of light and darkness. It is death that makes the difference, because in other city is death linked so closely to life: due to the coexistence and the continuous alteration of styles, various artistic forms of expression, manifestations of aristocratic opulence on the one hand and a dignified poverty on the other – all these features can be found alternating without a pattern of continuity in the façades of those palaces, shops, and houses which virtually nestle in their confined space.

In Ludes, the powerful, straight stroke connects palaces with churches, as a symbolic topos for transition and return, as a bridge between this world and the next. The graphic signs establish a relationship, a web with material and immaterial points of contact between the artist's energy and other energies which are floating through the sphere.

For this "cimmerio", Venice is the place of mystic and artistic contemplation; it is the beginning of a continuous metamorphosis which is Life. The black-and-white Venice of Guido Ludes is brought to life by the trembling affection of her creator and she receives material warmth through his hand. Venice marks the characteristic trait of an artist who finds himself on the search for eternal, lyrical values; Venice tells us of the mysterious relationship between man and the world of material objects, which is spiritualised and granted an ontological reality by him who names it.

"My Venice will not sink" is the title of one of Ludes's drawings – an imploring message that sounds like a promise.

NEVIA PIZZUL CAPELLO, VENICE

12

Die Straßen sind oft so eng,

daß kaum eine Person durchkann,

und wenn Mann und Weib sich einander begegnen,

so müssen sie sich mit den Rücken

nach den Mauern und vorn einander drücken,

bis jedes vorbei ist.

Wilhelm Heinse, Tagebücher

Le strade sono spesso così strette,

che vi si può passare solo a stento,

e quando uomo e donna qui s'incontrano

devono addossarsi ai muri,

sfiorandosi, fintanto che ciascuno sia passato.

Often, the streets are ever so narrow

that hardly anybody is able to get through,

and when man and woman happen to meet,

both have to press their backs to the walls

and their fronts against each other

until they have passed.

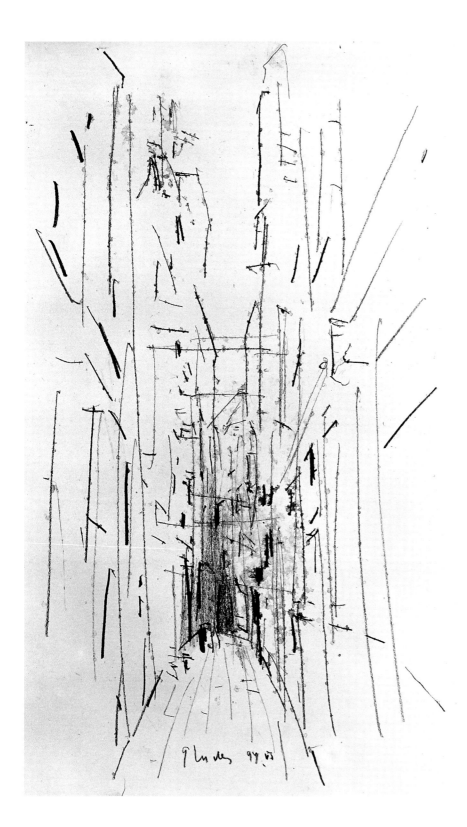

Wenn einst Venedig

       wieder in die Lagunen hinabgesunken sein mag,

    dann wird seine Geschichte

wie ein Nixenmärchen klingen...   **Dovesse un giorno Venezia**

    riaffondare nella laguna,

       la sua storia avrà l'eco di una fiaba ninfale..

Once Venice has gone down

    to the bottom of the lagoons again,

her history will sound like a nymph tale...

Heinrich Heine, Elementargeister, 1833

Wer am Markusplatz

sein Herz nicht schlagen fühlt,

hat keines.

Franz Grillparzer
Tagebuch auf der Reise nach Italien
1819

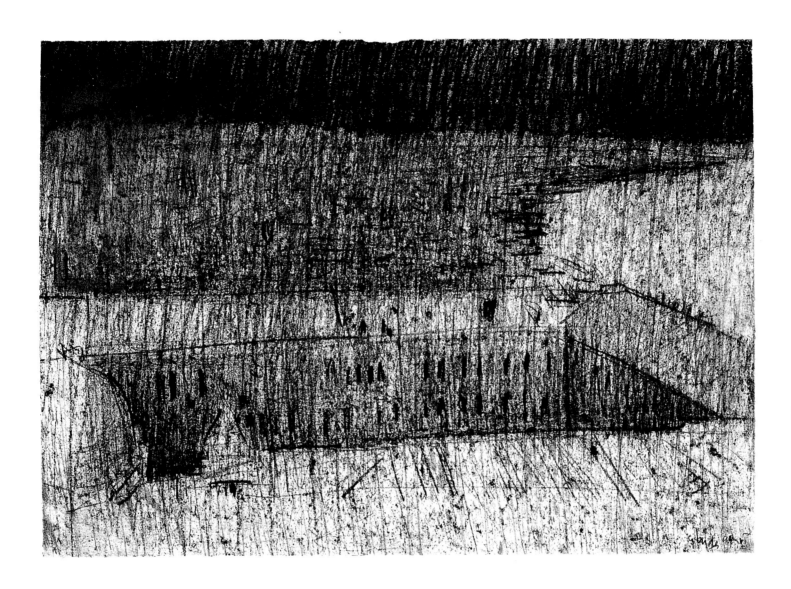

Chi, in piazza San Marco,

non sente battere il suo cuore,

non ha un cuore.

> Whoever does not feel
>
> his heart beating at St. Mark's Place,
>
> has no heart at all.

Die Zeit ist hin - doch weilt noch Schönheit hier...

Il tempo se ne è andato - ma la bellezza indugia ancora...

Those days are gone - but beauty is still here...

Lord G. G. N. Byron

34

Die gegenseitige Leidenschaft Venezias und des Herbstes,

die beide zum höchsten Gipfel ihrer sinnlich wahrnehmbaren Schönheit steigert,

hat ihre Ursache in einer tiefgehenden innerlichen Verwandtschaft:

Venedigs Seele, die Seele, mit der die alten Künstler die schöne Stadt bekleideten,

ist herbstlich.

> *...die Zweideutige zeigt uns die Möglichkeit eines Schmerzes,*
>
> *der sich verwandelt in anspornende, durchdringende Tatkraft...*

La mutua passione di Venezia e dell'Autunno

che esalta l'una e l'altro al sommo grado di lor bellezza sensibile,

ha origine in una affinità profonda;

poiché l'anima di Venezia, l'anima che foggiarono alla Città bella gli antichi artefici,

è autunnale.

> *...l'ambigua ci mostra la possibilità di un dolore*
>
> *trasmutato nella più efficace energia stimolatrice,*

Gabriele d'Annunzio, Il Fuoco

The mutual passion of Venice and her autumn,

which raises one and the other to the highest level of their delicate beauty,

has its origin in a profound affinity;

thus, the spirit of Venice,

the spirit which once animated the city through ancient artefacts,

this spirit is autumnal.

> *...this ambiguity reveals to us the feasibility of a pain*
>
> *which may be transmuted into a highly efficient,*
>
> *stimulating energy...*

Thomas Moore, Venetian Air

Unsere Barke, meine Liebe, ist nahe:

    nun dann, sie wird dich,

        während jene Wolken dort über dem Mond schweben,

La nostra barca, o amata, si avvicina:

sicher über die stille Lagune geleiten.

    ed ora, mentre le nubi veleggiano laggiù sopra la luna,

        ti porterà al sicuro, sulla silente laguna.

    Our bark, love, is near:

now, now while there hover those clouds over the moon,

    'twill waft thee safe over

    yon silent lagoon.

...immer noch hörst du die Kirchen erzählen;

Senti? Le chiese continuano a narrare;

doch die Paläste an stillen Kanälen

ma i palazzi su silenziosi canali restano muti.

Rainer Maria Rilke, Venedig

... you still hear the churches talking;

verraten nichts mehr.

but the palaces along the quiet canals

have gone silent.

Auf dem Canal Grande

Auf dem Canal Grande betten

Tief sich ein die Abendschatten,

Hundert dunkle Gondeln gleiten

Calano in fondo al Canal Grande

Als ein flüsterndes Geheimnis.

le ombre della sera,

scivolano cento gondole oscure,

segreto che fluisce in un bisbiglio.

On the Grand canal

        an evening shadow deeply embeds itself;
a hundred dark gondolas glide
    as a whispering mystery.

Conrad Ferdinand Meyer

Mit versagendem Ortssinn,

da die Gäßchen, Gewässer,

                                            E il senso dell'orientamento

Brücken und Plätzchen des Labyrinthes zu sehr einander gleichen...

                                            sembra venir meno,

                                            poiché le callette, i rii, i ponti

Die Gesänge,

    die man dort vernimmt,

    sind wachsende Klagen,

    die nicht aufsteigen

    und wie ein wallender Qualm

    über den Gassen lagern.

Le canzoni

    che là risuonano

    sono lamenti in crescendo,

    inetti a salire,

    che si adagiano sulle calli

    come un fluttuar di fumosi vapori.

The cantos

    you hear there

    are mounting wails

    which do not rise

    but lie over the narrow lanes

    like a surging smoke.

Rainer Maria Rilke
über das Ghetto von Venedig,
Geschichten vom Lieben Gott

Was ich träume, fragst du?

      Daß wir beide

Gestern starben und im weißen Kleide,

      Weiße Blumen in den losen Haaren,

  In der schwarzen Gondel meerwärts fahren...

Hermann Hesse, Venezianische Gondelgespräche

Che sogno, mi chiedi?

    Che ieri morivamo entrambi

      e, l'abito candido, candidi fiori tra i capelli disciolti,

sulla nera gondola, andavamo incontro al mare...

You wonder what I'm dreaming about?

    About the two of us

  Who died yesterday and who, in white garments,

With white flowers in our loose hair,

    Moved in a black gondola towards the sea...

Von den Euganeischen Hügeln, 11. Oktober 1797

    Unser Vaterland ist geopfert:

    Alles ist verloren...

    ich habe Venedig verlassen...

    weil ich an meinem Vaterland und mir verzweifle.

28. Oktober 1797

    ... es scheint mir unmöglich,

    daß unser Vaterland so zertreten wurde

    und uns noch ein Leben bleibt.

Da' colli Euganei, 11 Ottobre 1797

    Il sacrificio della patria nostra è consumato :

    tutto è perduto...

    ho lasciato Venezia...

    poiché ho disperato della mia patria e di me.

28 Ottobre 1797

    ...e' mi pare impossibile

    che la nostra patria sia così conculcata

    mentre ci resta ancora una vita.

Ugo Foscolo – Ultime lettere di Jacopo Ortis

From the Euganean Hills, 11 October 1797

    Our country's sacrifice has been consumed:

    all is lost...

    I have left Venice...

    for I feel I'm despairing of my country and of myself.

28 October 1797

    ...and I can hardly believe

    that our country is being oppressed like that

    while there is still another life left.

Die alten Paläste zerfrißt unser zeitgenössischer Atem...

Günter Kunert, Venedig I, 1978

Gli antichi palazzi intacca il nostro fiato contemporaneo

The old palaces are devoured by our contemporary spirit...

...die Gondeln gleiten,

    da die venezianischen Häuser bei Anbruch der Nacht durch Holzläden völlig verschlossen werden,

    außer durch Totenstille auch durch Totendunkel...

...poichè a Venezia,

    al calar della notte, le case serrano le loro imposte, le gondole scivolano in un silenzio di tomba,

    attraverso un buio di tomba..

...as the Venetian

    houses are completely closed up by their wooden shutters when night is falling

    the gondolas glide not only through deathly silence but also through deathly darkness...

Ernst Bloch, Venedigs italienische Nacht, 1934

Friedrich Nietzsche

Hundert tiefe Einsamkeiten

bilden zusammen die Stadt Venedig -

Cento profonde solitudini formano insieme la città di Venezia -

dies ist ihr Zauber.

Together, a hundred deep solitudes

questo è il suo fascino.

form the city of Venice -

this is her magic charm.

Ezra Pound, Night Litany, 1908

Und die Schönheit deiner Stadt Venedig

hast du mir dargetan

E la bellezza di questa tua Venezia

bis mir ihre Lieblichkeit in Tränen gerann.

me l'hai mostrata finchè la sua

amenità non mi si dissolse in pianto.

And the beauty of this thy Venice

hast thou shewn unto me

until is its loveliness become unto me

a thing of tears.

Biographie Guido Ludes

1949	*Geboren in Saarburg/Rheinland-Pfalz* *Studium „Graphik-Design" an der Fachhochschule* *Trier und „Kunstpädagogik"* *an der Johannes Gutenberg-Universität Mainz*
1980	*Förderpreis „Malerei" des Landes Rheinland-Pfalz*
1982	*Preis im Künstlerwettbewerb* *„Das Hambacher Fest"*
1984	*Daniel-Henry-Kahnweiler-Preis* *der Deutschen Kahnweiler-Stiftung* *Lincolnshire-Stipendium des Landes Rheinland-* *Pfalz*
1987	*Preis im Internationalen Kunstwettbewerb* *„Boehringer Ingelheim Kunstpreis" Brüssel/Belgien*
1992	*Preis im Landeswettbewerb* *„Kunst und Künstler in Rheinland-Pfalz"*
1994	*Professur für das Fach „Künstlerische Grafik" im* *Fachbereich Gestaltung der Fachhochschule* *Wiesbaden*
Seit 1976	*Einzelausstellungen in Deutschland und vielen* *europäischen Ländern sowie in den USA.* *Teilnahme an nationalen und internationalen* *Ausstellungen.*
Seit 1980	*Publikationen, Dokumentationen und Projekte* *„Kunst am Bau"* *Exkursionen nach Italien, Frankreich, Spanien,* *Island, Grönland, Schottland, Rußland, Türkei,* *Israel und Ägypten* *Mitglied verschiedener Künstlervereinigungen in* *Deutschland und Österreich* *Die Arbeiten von Guido Ludes befinden sich in* *zahlreichen öffentlichen und privaten Sammlungen* *des In- und Auslandes*

1949	Nato a Saarburg/Renania-Palatinato studio dell'arte grafica al politecnico di Treviri; poi, studio della pedagogia di belle arti all'università di Magonza	1949	Born in Saarburg/Rhineland-Palatinate educated at Trier Polytechnic of Art where he studied design, and at Mainz University where he took a degree in art education
1980	Premio di pittura della regione Renania-Palatinato (per promuovere gli artisti giovani)	1980	Rhineland-Palatinate Award for Painting (to foster young artists)
1982	Premio nel concorso d'artisti „La Festa d'Ambach" („Das Hambacher Fest")	1982	Prize at the Hambach Festival Art Competition („Das Hambacher Fest")
1984	Premio „Daniel-Henry-Kahnweiler" della Fondazione Kahnweiler di Germania, Borsa di studio „Lincolnshire" della regione Renania-Palatinato	1984	Daniel-Henry-Kahnweiler Award of the German Kahnweiler Foundation, Lincolnshire Scholarship of Rhineland-Palatinate
1987	Premio nel concorso internazionale d'artisti „Premio d'arte di Boehringer Ingelheim" („Boehringer Ingelheim Kunstpreis"); Bruxelles, Belgio	1987	Prize at the International Art Competition „Boehringer Ingelheim Prize for Art" („Boehringer Ingelheim Kunstpreis"); Brussels, Belgium
1992	Premio nel concorso regionale „L'arte e gli artisti in Renania-Palatinato" („Kunst und Künstler in Rheinland-Pfalz")	1992	Prize at the regional competition „Art and Artists in Rhineland-Palatinate" („Kunst und Künstler in Rheinland-Pfalz")
1994	Professorato di „Arte grafica" all'istituto „Creazione artistica" del politecnico di Wiesbaden	1994	Chair in „Artistic Design" („Künstlerische Grafik") at Wiesbaden Polytechnic, Department of Creation and Design („Gestaltung")
dal 1976	Esposizioni individuali e anche con altri artisti in Germania, in molti altri paesi europei e negli Stati Uniti d'America	since 1976	Solo exhibitions in Germany and many other European countries as well as in the U.S.A.; participation in both national and international exhibitions
dal 1980	Pubblicazioni, documentazioni e progetti „L'arte nella construzione" („Kunst am Bau") Viaggi di studio in Italia, Francia, Spagna, Islanda, Groenlandia, Scozia, Russia, Turchia, in Israele e in l'Egitto Membro di diverse associazioni d'artisti (in Germania ed Austria)	since 1980	Publications, documentations and projects „Art in Construction" („Kunst am Bau") Excursions to Italy, France, Spain, Iceland, Greenland, Scotland, Russia, Turkey, Israel and Egypt Member of various Artist Societies in Germany and Austria
	Le opere di Guido Ludes si trovano in numerose collezioni pubbliche e private all'interno ed all'estero		The works of Guido Ludes can be found in numerous public and private collections at home and abroad

Verzeichnis der Abbildungen

Seite					
Pagina					
Page					

02/03	Ereignis I	Avvenimento I	Event I	1995	60 x 80 cm
12/13	Nächtliche Salute	Salute notturno	Nightly Salute	1994	40 x 57,5 cm
15	Zur Piazza!	Alla Piazza!	To the Piazza!	1995	85 x 60 cm
16	Stadtlandschaft Venedig	Regione urbana Venezia	Townscape Venice	1995	40 x 57,5 cm
17	Gasse/Pesceria	Viuzza/Pesceria	Lane/Pesceria	1995	58 x 60 cm
18	Wintergasse in Venedig	Viuzza d'inverno a Venezia	Winter lane in Venice	1994	57,5 x 40 cm
19	Szene	Scena	Scene	1995	85 x 60 cm
21	C. G. Für Carlo Naya	C. G. A Carlo Naya	C. G. For Carlo Naya	1994	60 x 80 cm
22/23	Campanile S. Marco			1995	40 x 57,5 cm
24	Gondeltrauer	Gondola da lutto	Gondola of Mourning	1994	40 x 57,5 cm
25	P. D. und Riva I	P. D. e Riva I	P. D. and Riva I	1994	40 x 57,5 cm
26/27	San Marco und Dogenpalast I	San Marco e Palazzo Ducale I	San Marco and Doge's Palace	1994	40 x 57,5 cm
28	Piazetta			1995	40 x 57,5 cm
29	Basilica Fragment	Basilica Frammento	Basilica Fragment	1995	86 x 60,5 cm
30	Piazza San Marco			1994	40 x 57,5 cm
31	Nachtregen mit San Marco	Pioggia notturna con San Marco	Night Rain with San Marco	1994	40 x 57,5 cm
32/33	Mondnacht Februar	Notte lunare Febbraio	Moon Night February	1994	40 x 57,5 cm
34/35	Rialto			1995	60 x 80 cm
36/37	Canal Grande			1994	40 x 57,5 cm
38	Winter von Rialto	L'inverno da Rialto	Winter from Rialto	1994	42,5 x 29,5 cm
39	Venezianische Winterstimmung	Spirito d'inverno veneziano	Venetian Winter atmosphere	1995	57,5 x 40 cm
40/41	Später/ Januarnacht I	Piú tardi/ Notte di Gennaio I	Later/ January Night I	1994	40 x 57,5 cm
42	Am Canal	Sul canale	At the Canal	1995	57,5 x 40,5 cm
44 A	Ponte			1994	57,5 x 40 cm
44 B	Nachtgang IV	Passeggiata notturna IV	Night Walk IV	1995	57,5 x 40 cm
45	Rio			1994	57,5 x 40 cm
46	Nacht	Notte	Night	1994	57,5 x 40 cm
47	Giudecca-Regen	Giudecca-Pioggia	Giudecca-Rain	1995	85 x 60 cm

Seite	48	Januar-Abend – Venedig	Sera di Gennaio – Venezia	Evening in January – Venicie	1995	85 x 60	cm
Pagina					1995	85 x 60	cm
Page	49	Campo			1994	57,5 x 40	cm
	50/51	Campo			1995	60 x 80	cm
	53	Nacht	Notte	Night	1995	57,5 x 40	cm
	54/55	Ereignis II	Avvenimento II	Event II	1995	60 x 80	cm
	56/57	Salute Studie II	Salute Schizzo II	Salute Sketch II	1994	40 x 57,5	cm
	58/59	Salute II, III, VI, V			1994	40 x 57,5	cm
	61	Nacht am großen Kanal	Notte sul Canal Grande	Night at the Grand Canal	1995	60 x 80	cm
	62	Salute			1994	57,5 x 40	cm
	63	Ponte			1995	85 x 60	cm
	65	Gassenregen im Dorsoduro	Viuzza, piovosa nel Dorsoduro	Rainy Lane in the Dorsoduro	1995	85 x 60	cm
	66	Ghetto			1995	85 x 60	cm
	68	Irgendwo in Venedig	In qualche posto di Venezia	Somewhere in Venice	1995	60 x 80	cm
	69	Campo			1994	40 x 57,5	cm
	70	Turm	Torre	Campanile	1994	57,5 x 40	cm
	71	S. Polo Winter	S. Polo Inverno	S. Polo Winter	1995	57,5 x 40	cm
	72	Salute I			1994	40 x 57,5	cm
	73	Salute spät	Salute tardo	Salute late	1995	57,5 x 40	cm
	74/75	Salute-Regen	Salute-Pioggia	Salute-Rain	1994	40 x 57,5	cm
	77	Nachtgang Giudecca	Passeggiata notturna Giudecca	Night Walk Giudecca	1995	57,5 x 40	cm
	78	Venedig Ensemble	Ensemble veneziano	Venetian Ensemble	1995	40 x 57,5	cm
	79	Großer Nachtgang	Grande passeggiata notturna	Great Night Walk	1995	85 x 60	cm
	81	Regen	Pioggia	Rain	1995	60 x 80	cm
	83	Für Carlo Ponti	A Carlo Ponti	For Carlo Ponti	1995	57,5 x 40	cm
	84/85	Später/ Januarnacht II	Più tardi/ Notte di Gennaio II	Later/ January Night II	1994	40 x 57,5	cm
	86	Cimitero S. Michele			1994	40 x 57,5	cm
	87	S. Michele II			1995	57,5 x 40	cm
	88	Erstes letztes Vaporetto	Primo ultimo vaporetto	First last Vaporetto	1995	85 x 60	cm
	90/91	Santa Maria della Salute			1994	40 x 57,5	cm

Impressum

Herausgeber	Michael Reitzel
Gestaltung	Gregor Krisztian
Textredaktion	Hermann Kurzke
Vorwort	Nevia Pizzul Capello
Übersetzungen	Christiane Wenz / Nevia Pizzul Capello
Koordination	Sieglinde Ludes
Fotos	Silke Bartsch / Isolde Luckert
Lithografie	Saase & Heller Reprotechnik GmbH, Ingelheim
Satz	Gesetzt aus der Caecilia Roman Italic und Franklin Gothic Demi
Papier	Gedruckt auf holzfrei weiß matt gestrichen chlorfrei Bilderdruck „Phönomatt", 150 g/m^2
Gesamtherstellung	Universitätsdruckerei und Verlag H. Schmidt GmbH, Mainz
Buchbinderische Verarbeitung	C. Fikentscher GmbH, Darmstadt

© 1996
Verlag Hermann Schmidt Mainz
und Guido Ludes Mainz
Alle Rechte vorbehalten

Die Deutsche Bibliothek –
CIP-Einheitsaufnahme

Ludes, Guido:
Venedig = Venezia / Guido Ludes.
Mit einem Vorw. von Nevia Pizull Capello.
Textausw. von Hermann Kurzke.
Hrsg. von Michael Reitzel.
[Übers.: Christiane Wenz / Nevia Pizull Capello]. –
Mainz : Schmidt, 1996

ISBN 3-87439-383-6